"Tips" and "Tools"

for a

Safe and Healthy School Year

by Patrice Lee

"You Just Needed Love"

You made me realize how special I was.
There was something I had
. . . something you wanted,
. . . something you needed,
. . . something you found in me.

There was something in your life

. . . that you were lacking,
. . . you were looking for,
. . . you were searching for,
. . . Bully, you just needed

...LOVE!!

Table of Contents

Preface

We live during a time when some students attack other students simply because they don't like the other students. The attackers may even jump on their victims in front of that person's parents. This is a time when children are attempting to, and committing suicide because of fear. Many parents are looking for answers, while others are wondering what happened.

Parents and children can be safe and healthy if they make a conscientious effort to do so, but they must not walk around as though blindfolded. Because we are living in perilous times, responsible parents and like-minded adults, must walk in their authority, respecting self and others, in a concerted effort to provide protection for their children's emotional and physical well-being.

Since bullying is a major problem, let's look at some "tips and tools" that can help parents who are looking for answers.

Introduction

There are many types of bullies and many reasons children and adults are bullied. In this book you'll find tips for identifying the child who has been bullied, and some tips to help remove the barriers or roadblocks to good communication between parent and child.

The author shares how to avoid the negative effects of bullies, including, the "name-calling" and "cyber" bullies found in the classroom, on the playground, around the school and on the internet. You will also find parent tips, family tips and survival tips for adult bully victims (especially at the workplace), as well as seven things to consider before you send that text message.

If you are a parent who needs to be encouraged, this is the right book for you. If your children need to be encouraged "Tips & Tools" can help them too.

Let's make this school year and the ones that follow the best school year ever for children, youth, and parents.   Let's bring families together to save lives, and help the bullies too.

Now, you might ask, "What is a bully?" Let's begin with my personal definition.

B - A boy or girl, (man or woman)

U - with unresolved issues that cause
     them to have

L - loud outbursts, expressing anger,
     producing fear in others, mostly due to a

L - lack of love;

Y - yearning attention.

"TIPS"

The "tips and tools" in this book can be used at any stage in life – from the preschooler to the adult. They promote excellence in health for the mind, body and soul; for as one thinks, so he becomes.

Encourage your children to think positively. Let your youth know that their future is not dictated by naysayers or mean-spirited people, but that their future is bright. Let them know that they are what they "think and say" they are; and that what they "say and think" is ultimately, what they become.

Children also need to hear their parents speak positively of them on a regular basis. The following statements are the kind of words your children need to hear. "In my book, you are the head, not the tail. You are above only, not beneath. You are first, not last. And you have the ability to excel in every area of your life, for you are a winner, not a loser."

Tell your teenagers, "I believe in you, and I look forward to your accomplishments and successes in life. I expect you to have positive outcomes despite any challenges you may face, and I believe you will experience one victory after another."

The words that I share are the same words I had to say to myself. I repeated them as often as needed until I began to experience one victory after another in my life. No matter what it looked like, I kept talking, because, sometimes you just have to encourage yourself. And sometimes, you may be all you've got.

As you apply this information to your life, let your children and youth know that no bully can stop them from achieving their goals and becoming who they are called to be.

I am ready for a wonderful school year. How about you?

With bullying on the rise, parents may find that their children need extra encouragement, whether they are attending a new school, or going to school for the first time. So let's look at some "tips" for the new school attendees.

"New School"
Bully Awareness Tips

~

If your children are entering a new school:

1. Talk to them about this new experience

2. Tell to them to expect everything to be different and to look at this experience as an opportunity to make new friends

3. Encourage them to talk with you each day. Best times to talk: Right after school. Listen attentively, and let them know you are interested in what they are saying.

4. Get to know the principal, teacher and counselors right away.

5. Participate in parent organizations such as the Parent Teacher Association, PTO, etc.

6. Give your children lots of hugs.

Work with the Law

~ To make the world a safer place for us all ~

1. Know where your local police precinct is, and how to get there.

2. Keep the precinct phone number handy.

3. Attend community meetings at your local precinct, if they have them.

4. Always respect law enforcement officers and obey the rules/laws of your local, state and federal government.

5. Make sure you understand the law. If you're not sure, ask. The knowledge gained could save your life or the life of someone else.

6. Be a friend to the law enforcement agencies in your area by getting involved with community projects supported by local officers.

7. Be informed. Be safe.

8. Show a little kindness.   When you see
   a police officer, sergeant, lieutenant,
   commander, or commander in chief,
   take a moment to thank him for his
   service.

9. Pray for his/her safety.

How well do you know the law as it relates to bullying in your area?

It's important to know the laws of your city and state on bullying. You may want to contact your state's Department of Justice for the latest information.

Healthy Mind -- > = Healthier
Better You

"Day-Maker Tip"

You can have a great day every day, if you begin each day with a grateful heart:

1. Wake up and decide to be happy every day. Keep a song in your heart.

2. Begin each day with prayer, welcoming Jesus into your day. He wants you hear from you, and to have you spend quality time with Him.*

3. Eat a healthy breakfast, lunch and dinner.

4. Think positive thoughts all day.

5. Get plenty of exercise daily.

6. Smile often. Let it become a habit. You'll be pleased to know that others will begin to smile back at you.

7. Memorize a verse of scripture from The Bible, a Proverb, or your favorite verse to remain positive.

8. Forgive instantly. It will help you heal faster.

9. Expect to have a peaceful day. :)

Extra Tip: God loves variety, and He made fruits and vegetables of every color, to nourish our bodies and keep us strong. Eating more fresh fruit and vegetables, and less junk food will help us live healthier longer!

"A happier state of mind leads to a healthier state of mind"

* Many people call on Him only when they're in trouble. :(

Parent Tips:

For Children and Youth

10 Tips - Symptoms of a Bullied Child/Youth

These symptoms may be an indication that your child has been bullied.

1. Your child has a sudden change in personality or disposition; is irritable.
2. Your child may become withdrawn.
3. Your child has a change in posture, from good to a humped-over stance.
4. Your child gives unusual responses to your inquiries/does not respond at all.
5. Your child does not want to go to school.
6. Your child has a loss of appetite.
7. Your child can't express his feelings.
8. Your child becomes disruptive in school.
9. Your child experiences a change in sleeping habits; or has insomnia.
10. Your child becomes explosive or overwhelmed with emotions.

(What to Do) If Your Child Has Been Bullied

So often, innocent children and youth are mistreated by mean-spirited people, just because they happen to be present. Your child could be an innocent bystander, or simply passing by at that particular moment.

In many instances, the encounter can't be avoided, because it is just happenstance. But, for those instances where it can be avoided, where a behavior is repeated intentionally, again and again, it is important to intervene in a responsible way on your child's behalf.

Here are 10 things to keep in mind:

1. Don't panic!!!
2. Do take immediate action.

3. Let your child know that he/she is loved. Tell him/her as often as needed.
4. Demonstrate love in your actions and deeds.
5. Report the incident to the principal or governing authority for the appropriate action to be taken. Continue to follow-up, until the problem is resolved.
6. Encourage your child to share what happened/talk about the incident.
7. Assure your child of your support. Stay positive when communicating with your child.
8. Keep your child engaged in activities that he/she enjoys.
9. Be very patient. The healing process may take some time if it has gone on for a duration.
10. Seek professional counseling, if needed.

~

In everything involving children, love should be the key ingredient. Did you know that perfect love erases fear? Jesus is perfect love.

~

Children and Youth:
Surviving a Bully's Negative Effects

Everyone knows that bullies are troublemakers. And they can cause all kinds of havoc in your life and really throw you off course.

That is why it is important to have the proper mindset, where you allow nothing to steal your peace. After all, you deserve to have a peaceful day, every day.

Let's look at some of the things you can do to practice safety, and maintain peace in your life, even if a bully decides to come your way.

Bully Safety Tips
(For your child/youth)

1. Avoid remote or hidden areas, and the area where you last encountered the bully. Keep your distance.

2. It is a good thing to ignore the bully if you can, by simply walking away.

3. You can throw the bully off, by asking questions, changing the subject, or saying something positive.

4. Take a positive stand by letting the bully know how you feel about what he/she is doing.

5. Walk or travel in multiples with friends and classmates who offer their support.

6. Practice non-violence. Choose to walk in forgiveness.

7. Report every occurrence of bullying right away to parent, teacher, principal, counselor or another responsible adult.

8. Record dates and times of all bully activity, and all witnesses.

9. Depending on the severity of the bully attack, you may need to file a police report.

10. Overcome the feeling of rejection with laughter. Laugh at the bully's comment about you and laugh out loud. It will defeat his (her) purpose.

There are many more things you can do. Always keep it positive, and encourage peace.

"For God has not given us the spirit of fear, but of power, and of love, and of a sound mind" (2 Timothy 1:7).

"Nurturing a Bully"
{Parents Beware}

~

When I asked a first-grader to define
"bully."
She said, "A bully is a hater."

~

"Bully-Type" Children

Children who are bullies need love, just like everyone else. Sometimes, however, this key ingredient is missing from the home of the bully-type child. And sometimes the love a parent gives is misguided. May I speak the truth in love?

The truth is: Buying your children everything they want or ask for is not a true demonstration of love. The next few pages are written specifically for that overindulgent parent. Please read on. . .

"Don't Ignore the Problem, You Could Be Creating a Bully"

While you are in search of answers, you may be overlooking the problem. So often, and for many reasons, parents ignore the signs of trouble at onset. Perhaps they could be too tired to notice, preoccupied from the events of the day, or too busy with other things.

As soon as you notice that your child is having sudden outbursts, or displaying aggressive behavior, address the issue. This kind of behavior can lead to one or more bully-types. It could be that your child has been bullied, and is afraid to talk about it.

In fact, the bullying may be ongoing. If your child's unruly behavior continues, you should seek professional counseling right away. The sooner you address the change in your child's behavior, the greater the odds will be for immediate healing to occur and the recovery from damages.

In a calm, firm voice you might say to your child/youth:

1. "Your behavior is unacceptable."

2. "Let's talk about what's bothering you?"

3. "Are you hurt?" "Are you in pain?"

4. "Did someone harm you (physically, or verbally) in any way?"

5. "What are you trying to tell me?"

6. "I'm concerned about you. Let's talk.?"

7. "Tell me what's on your mind?"

If Your Son/Daughter is the Bully...

Then it's important that you:

1. Identify the root cause of the problem.
2. Talk with your child.
3. When your child begins to share – Listen.
4. Calmly respond using few words. Keep your sentences/questions short.
5. Don't jump to conclusions.
6. Give your child a reasonable amount of time to work thru the issues.
7. Have your child apologize (to the victim) for their actions.
8. Be firm and consistent with your instruction as you walk the love walk.
9. Pray with, and for your child daily.
10. Get professional counseling, youth minister, pastor, etc., if needed.

Establishing and Building Trust Between You and Your Child

When you speak:

1. Say what you mean. And mean it when you say it. Be consistent.
2. Speak truth, and expect it in return.

By your actions:

3. Do what you say you are going to do.
4. When you make a promise to your child, keep it.
5. Love your child unconditionally.
6. Be kind to your neighbors.
7. Walk in a spirit of forgiveness.
8. Be a good role model.
9. Teach your child to trust in God. Be his example.
10. Think on things that are honest, lovely and just.
11. Display love in all that you do – children are observing.

Important Parent Note: Parents need to know what a child experiences during the school day. Sometimes your child needs to feel your presence at school. The more involved you are, the more you will be able to relate to and understand your child's needs.

Lavatories and hallways are danger zones. In some middle and high schools, they have become the scene of violence during the course of the day. Here's a suggestion: If your child's school does not have one, you might consider organizing a parent volunteers group to help during the school day.

Having parent volunteers present between 10:00a.m. and 2:00p.m., could have a great effect on the school climate, and might greatly reduce the occurrence of violence in those key areas.

CELL Phones

"Can You Hear Me Now?"

Can you imagine being without it for day? Most people go back home to get their cell phone when they realize they don't have it. Yes, once you have one, you don't want to be without it.

CELL PHONES:
Consider and Reconsider

What is the appropriate age for a child to have a cell phone?

This is something that varies in every family for each child. But I will give you some things to think about.

You may want to consider the following:

Does your child do all of his/her chores without reminders? Does your child remember to, or make an effort to complete all of his homework without reinforcements.

Has your child proven he/she is responsible enough to handle a cell phone and all that comes with it? And finally, have you shared everything you want your son/daughter to know before you expose him/her to this powerful mode of communication?

Now reconsider and evaluate the maturity level of your child, and think about the childlike ways of your innocent children before you say "yes."

You must decide for your family what is age appropriate, but here are some things to consider for your younger children:

The longer you wait, the less problems or concerns you'll have with text and cyber-bullying. This is true if you're instilling discipline in your child, and exercising restraints against excessive computer use.

As I mentioned earlier, these are just a few things for you as a responsible parent to consider.

"Toddler Tips"
(On cell phone usage)

The cell phone is not a gadget or toy, so we encourage you to stick with the basics.   When it comes to babies and toddlers, they need food, clothing, shelter and lots of "love."

Never let your toddler go to sleep with a cell phone or any type of technology. Young children should have toy phones.

You can help your toddler develop a love for reading, by reading to him each night. They need to hear bed time stories, then have you tuck them in real tight.

Stuffed animals and dolls, trucks and tee ball will help them be children. Playing with other children will help them develop social skills, and learn to get along with others.

Don't you love to see children play?

So You Have a Cell Phone. . .

Do you remember how you felt when you got your first cell phone? It was an experience that brought great joy.

You wanted to hold a conversation with your family, friends and loved ones. You also wanted to know how far your calls could go, and to let everyone know that you had a cell phone. Oh, how important this cell phone made you feel.

Well, nothing has changed about those first feelings. They occur every time a child, teen or adult receives his/her first cell phone. But, it's different now, because technology has turned the cell phone into a tiny computer that can do so much more than help you hold a conversation with a friend.

That is the reason we offer these tips for proper etiquette, so we don't offend our friends and neighbors in cyber space.

7 Tips to Consider Before You Text

Children and youth are allowed to have cell phones at an early age. With the cell phone comes additional responsibility.

So children must be taught to be responsible. Here are some questions children must ask themselves before sending a text message. It works for adults too.

Ask yourself:

1. Do I have the right phone number?
2. Is this message worth repeating? Does it have value?
3. Is it necessary?
4. Is it uplifting?
5. Is the message timely?
6. Is my message clear? Is it accurate?
7. Will it shed a positive light on others?

7 Tips to Safeguard You from the "Text-Bully"

If you have been a victim of text/cyber bullying, this time you might want to use caution before sharing your new number with all of your friends. Here are some suggestions:

1. Weed out your so-called friends.
2. Selectively decide who deserves to have your (cell phone) information, before you change your phone number.
3. Report any form of threatening or distressful messages (texts/photos/videos) and move on.
4. Treat your cell phone as "private property" – Put up the "No Trespassing" sign.
5. Avoid contact with the "text bully" to avoid argumentation.
6. Cut your ties to the messenger once you have made the police report. Have no future communication with them.
7. Try not to take it personally - it could be the wrong number.

"Text/Cyber-bullying"
A Tip for the Cyber Victim

If you have been a victim of cyber-bullying and have had to alter your daily routines because of the reaction of friends or those you associate with, or if you are having repercussions because of it, here are two ways in which you might address the problem in an attempt to bring closure:

1. You may need to report the incident to your local law enforcement authorities.
2. Send a response to those persons who received the information, via social media or text.

You might say something like this:

"I selectively choose not to address the matter other than to say I ...forgive my offender for the damage he (she) has caused me by way of offense from slanderous statements and false accusations made against me, and for the embarrassment it may have brought.

I will use extreme caution in who I allow to be in my inner circle of friends or close associates from this day forth. More importantly, I refuse to render evil for evil. I submit this matter to God, for I know He cares about what concerns me. I know He can handle it, for He said 'Vengeance is mine. I will repay.' "

Home "SWEET" Home

~

Be grateful for every blessing that
comes your way.

~

"Creating a Stress-Free Environment @ Home"

Everyone has quirks or shortcomings. So, why not teach your child to be good-natured about his/hers? You can do this by example.

1. Be a great example, even when it comes to your shortcomings. It's okay to admit that you have shortcomings, because no one is perfect.

2. Practice lighthearted humor at home. Learn to smile/laugh at some of your mishaps. This will help your child to not take everything so seriously.

3. Instead of being upset about something you didn't do well, you might say, "I'll do better next time" or "I've learned something new." And say it with a smile.

4. Teach your child to expect something positive from each adversity.

5. Express the importance of the lesson learned from the adversity or mishap.

6. Keep the home atmosphere relaxed. Fill it with love, joy, peace and kindness. Let it be a place where you can unwind after a long or busy day. Set aside some time to play together.

~

"Love never fails"

~

<u>Note</u>: Children need encouraging words and words of praise. On page 89 of "Mommy, Are You Listening???" I share 100 ways you can praise your children to greatness.

"Family Tip"

Did you know that children who pray with their parents before they go to school usually have a happy ending to their day?

1. Create and maintain a loving atmosphere at home

2. Praise your child for every good deed or action of obedience

3. Offer "praise more" often than 'criticism (Better yet, don't criticize)

4. Spend less time on the computer/phone, and more time communicating with each other.

5. Have meals together

6. Laugh and play together

7. Pray always with, and for each other.

8. Encourage sibling support not rivalry. Love is helping one another.

Family is important to God. If you love
Jesus you are a member of God's
family.

Tips for Adults

~

Don't worry about the haters who never wish you well. Be Happy!

~

Overcoming Workplace Bullies

Now this one's a little tough, because sometimes the bully is your boss; and most times colleagues/co-workers won't befriend you because of their fear of receiving the same mistreatment you're receiving. Therefore, you must build your inner strength by relying on, and trusting in God to bring you through.

1. Get plenty of rest every night, so you can wake up refreshed every day.
2. Have a positive attitude each day
3. Remember to hold your head up. (The bully wants to see you discouraged.)
4. Keep accurate records, dates and times. Be an exemplary employee.
5. Ask God for grace to sustain you and

believe that change is coming.

6. Ask God for wisdom.

7. Remain calm.

8. Meditate on and believe God's Word. Apply specific promises to your life.

9. Be kind to others.

10. Encourage someone else in a similar position as yourself. It will help you to stop thinking about your problem.

11. And never, never give up

8 "Survival" Tips for Adult Bully Victims

If the bullying is continuous, you may need to use these survival tips until it ceases, especially if your boss is the bully. You should:

1. Maintain low visibility. The very sight of you could trigger an attack. Have you heard the expression, 'out of sight, out of mind?'
2. If possible, ignore it.
3. When the darts (harsh words) are thrown at you, keep moving. Have a "dodge ball" mindset.
4. Surround yourself with positive affirmations.
5. Always look pleasant. Wear a smile.
6. Have several good laughs each day.
7. Do something nice for yourself often.
8. Pray for your enemies, and forgive instantly.

Overcome Your Obstacles So You Can Help Your Child

1. Know that you can overcome any problem or circumstance
2. You must be willing to forgive, love and respect self first
3. Change your mind-set. Refresh your thoughts. Think positively.
4. Take responsibility for your actions, and think before you respond.
5. Be an example of love in action.
6. Know that nothing is impossible with God. And know that. . .

You can do it!

"TOOLS"

"TOOLS"

"Tools" are used to help you repair things, put things in order or make them right. Mechanics and repairmen are often recognized by the tools that they carry. Tools help you fix what is broken, repair leaks, mend, patch things up or maintain what you have.

Some tools are known for their sharpness. Some are known for their strength. Other tools and equipment are known for their power. The tools that I use are known for all of the above. They are strengthening, powerful and sharp.

These "tools" will bring peace and restore order in your life, and cause you to look at life's circumstances in a new perspective. These "tools" will help you keep a positive attitude, necessary for a healthy state of mind. But, even more, these tools can be activated at any time, for they are alive. I use the promises of God's Word as my "tool" for life.

Yes, you can apply the Word of God to your life, and change your life for good. I pray that you will experience many victories, as you apply the awesome promises of His Word to your life as well.

The "Tools" That I Used

Now that you have some tips, here are the tools that worked for me. Because of my personal relationship with Jesus, I was able to take the promises in His Word (The Holy Bible) and apply them to my life as needed.

Applying Your Tools

God's Word is alive and full of power. And Jesus is the same, yesterday, today, and forever. He does not change. The most wonderful thing about God's promise(s) is that He is no respecter of persons. If He did it for one person, He will do the same for you, according to your faith.

The only requirement is for you to believe, and not doubt. That means there's no room for fear either. Therefore, if we apply the Word of God to our problem, whatever it might be, and remind Him of His promise to us, He will do exactly what His Word says.

Oh, this is so exciting to me, because I have done just that. I have taken my concerns to Him, the problems, the obstacles, the bills and the bullies, and He resolved them; all of them. His Word, which He has spoken, never returns back unto Him void of power. If He said it, He will do it for you.

And oh, how He loves details. So be specific about whatever it is you need, want, or desire and apply His Word or His promise to that thing. And when it comes down to the bully, let God handle it for you. After all, He said, "Vengeance is mine. I will repay." (If I were you, I'd feel sorry for the bully, because after all is said and done, the bully's arms are too short to box with God.) **:)** I'm just sayin' "Bully beware."

Seven Steps to Victory

Here are seven steps:

1. Forgive those who have come against you, and forgive instantly.

2. Find the promise (in The Bible) that you want to believe God for in your life.

3. Say (read) His promise(s) out loud.

4. Refuse to doubt, and believe that what you have said will come to pass in your life.

5. Because you believe it, you can thank Him in advance. This will activate your faith.

6. You will feel an incredible amount of peace that follows this kind of faith.

 7. Others will notice the change in your life and wonder what you are doing.

Now, if you don't have a personal relationship with Jesus, you can invite Him into your heart and life right now. Then He will fulfill His promises for you just like He has for me. Please accept His invitation and say this out loud.

"Dear Heavenly Father, in the name of Jesus, I come to you today to give you my life. I ask for forgiveness of my sins and to be cleansed from all unrighteousness. I believe you sent your only Son, Jesus to die on the cross for my sins, and that He arose on the third day that I might be saved, and because of that I am right now, born again in Jesus Name. Amen.

If you've prayed this prayer, you can activate His tools in your life. And you can expect God to do as He has promised, for His promises never return unto Him void. He will do just what He said, as it is written, as you live for Him. Now keep reading to learn how to apply these Word tools to your life.

For Jesus says:

"Be not afraid, only believe..." (Mark 5:36)

Application of "The Word" Tools

When a parent wants to emphasize something important to their child, he/she usually repeats it several times until he is sure that child "gets it." God uses that same technique with us. Many times He repeats a promise to us several times, so we'll know that He means it, and that we understand how important it is.

In this section, I will give you the promises of God that I stood on, and my understanding of them as it applied to my situation. Here are some examples of how I used the Word as a tool to help me win the battle with the bullies and some of the other obstacles in my life.

Winning didn't mean that people could always see my victory. Since my bullies were all adults, winning meant being able to keep a positive attitude through a difficult situation, knowing that God would give me peace regardless of what was going on all around me.

For "courage and strength" I read and applied the following:

". . .be strong and of good courage; be not afraid, neither be thou dismayed; for the Lord thy God is with thee wherever thou goest" (Joshua 1:9). When God gives a promise, and wants to make sure we get it, sometimes He'll repeat the same key words three times consecutively, as He does in Joshua 1: vs. 6, 7, and 9. In this verse He says, "Be strong and of a good courage:" in verse 6a, "Only be thou strong and very courageous," 7a, and 9 of the same chapter. He seriously does not want us to be discouraged nor afraid, because He has our back.

My favorite Bible verse as a child was found in Psalm 46:1, "God is our refuge and strength, a very present help in trouble." I had no idea that this scripture would carry me through life, but it did. God is, indeed, my refuge and strength, and a very present help in trouble. I have certainly depended on Him for strength, each time trouble came my way.

He doesn't want us to be anxious about anything either. This is what God says about it. "Be anxious for nothing..." (Philippians 4:6a); and "Be still, and know that I am God..." (Psalm 46:10) This means don't be concerned about it. Just hold on and let God handle it. You need to understand that Jesus is full of love, joy and peace.

He said, "These things I command you, that ye love one another" (John 15:11) Love, love, love. He commands us to do this His way. God is love. And if we love Him, then it should be so reflective in our lives that others can see it. He repeated the command to love here: "Let us love one another, for love is of God" (1 John 4:7).

Did you know that God also wants you to be full of joy? King David knew this when he wrote, "You will show me the path that leads to life; for in thy presence is fullness of joy. . ." (Psalm 16:11b). If we stay in His presence we will be full of joy. In John 15:11b, Jesus said, ". . . that my (His) joy might remain in you, and that your joy might be full." Jesus really wants us to be happy.

Jesus told His disciples "Let not your heart be troubled..." in John 14:1a. What Jesus said to the disciples, can also be applied to us today. This Word is for us in our time of trouble or despair. Jesus said, "Peace I leave with you, my peace I give unto you; not as the world giveth, give I unto you. Let not your heart be troubled, neither let it be afraid" (John 14:27). And the promise of more peace, "And the peace of God, which passeth all understanding, shall keep your hearts and minds through Christ Jesus "(Philippians 4:7). God's peace will sustain you. God did it for me; I have His peace. And He has promised to keep me in "perfect peace. . ." (Isaiah 26:3) if I keep my mind stayed on Him.

There are many scriptures on fear, because God doesn't want us to "fear" or be afraid of anything. Now this is one verse I used often. "For God hath not given us the spirit of fear, but of power, of love, and of a sound mind" (2 Timothy 1:7).   It keeps me grounded.   And He tells us that "There is no fear in love, . . .perfect love casteth out fear. . ." (1 John 4:18a). There is absolutely "no fear" in love.

There are so many wonderful promises that I cannot share them all, but here are a few more that I made personal for my situation:

"Vengeance is mine; I will repay, saith the Lord" (Romans 12:19b).

"No weapon that is formed against me shall prosper, and every tongue that shall rise against me in judgment thou shalt condemn" (taken from Isaiah 54:17a).

"Fret not thyself because of evildoers, neither be thou envious against the workers of iniquity. For they shall soon be cut down like the grass, and wither as the green herb. Trust in the Lord, and do good. . ." (Psalm 37: 1-3a).

You will "...overcome them: because greater is He that is in you (me), than He that is in the world" (1 John 4:4b).

Now here's the promise that took me to the finish line. When my enemies would not let up, and I thought I couldn't handle it anymore, I opened my Bible to a passage in Isaiah I had never seen nor read before, and **Wow!!!** These are the words that spoke directly to me.

"Fear thou not; for I am with thee. Be not dismayed; for I am thy God. I will strengthen thee; yea, I will help thee; yea, I will uphold thee with the right hand of my righteousness. Behold, all they that were incensed against thee shall be ashamed and confounded: they shall be as nothing; and they that strive with thee shall perish. Thou shalt seek them, and shalt not find them, even them that contended with thee: they that war against thee, shall be as nothing and as a thing of nought. For I the Lord thy God will hold thy right hand, saying unto thee, Fear not; I will help thee" (Isaiah 41:10-13)

This scripture needed no interpretation for me. I got it the first time I read it. The message is so important in these verses that God said it again a few verses later. "Fear not; I will help thee" (Isaiah 41:13), and again, "Fear not, . . .I will help thee. . ." (Isaiah 41:14). Here is the same promise "...I will be with thee. . ." (Isaiah 43:2); and a reinforcement of the promise "Fear not: for I am with thee. . ." (Isaiah 43:5a).

He also said, "Fear not: for. . .thou art mine." (Isaiah 43:1b). Thank God for His unfailing love. He was not going to let me be destroyed by my enemies, for He had my back. The battle was over. 'And the winner is...' ☺

Jesus is the answer! And we always win with Him. For He said "I am the way, the truth, and the life: no man cometh unto the Father, but by me." (John 14:6). Oh, He loves you so much. If you only knew how much Jesus loves you.

'I will cast my care upon Him, for I know He cares about me.' Therefore, I will worry about nothing. (Refer to 1 Peter 5:7)

More Tools

for School, Work and Home

So, when it seems like things are getting too tough for you, just say these verses:

~ "He has girded me with strength unto the battle: and subdued under me those that rose up against me" (Found in Psalm 18:39).

~ "...The Lord is the strength of my life; of whom shall I be afraid?" (Psalm 27:1b).

~ "...in the time of trouble He shall hide me... be lifted up above my enemies..."(Ps. 27:5-6).

~ "...Let us love one another: for love is of God..." (1John 4:7a). "...Perfect love casteth out {destroys} fear..." (1 John 4:18b)

~ "I can do all things through Christ who strengthens me." (Philippians 4:13).

Now, you must "...only believe" (Mark 5:36).

And "...Fear not: believe only..." (Luke 8:50).

"Girded" – to encircle or bind with a flexible band; to equip (*Thefreedictionary.com*)

Bully-Free Pledge

(children and youth)

I pledge and promise:

1. To treat others with respect at all times.
2. To tell my parents or responsible adult immediately, if I have been bullied.
3. To tell a responsible adult, if I see someone being bullied.
4. To be a good role model for younger children and not engage in bully activity in any form.
5. To remain alert and cautious in unsupervised areas at school, such as, restrooms, hidden corridors and dark stairwells.
6. To show support to others who have been bullied.

"...for I am a remarkable individual, a gifted student, with a promising future. I am a reflection of the beauty that is bubbling up on the inside of me. And I choose to live my life bully-free."

Parent Promise

I Promise:

1. I will love each child "unconditionally."

2. I will feed my children less junk food and add more fruit and vegetables to their diet, so they can be healthier and have a greater capacity to learn.

3. I will give my children spiritual food to feed their faith and discourage fear, worry and doubt.

4. I will be an example of love, in action, at all times.

5. I will pray with and for my children before they go to school.

"Unconditionally" – without conditions or limitations; absolute   *Thefreedictionary.com*

Final TIP: **Do's & Don'ts**

Do:

1. Demonstrate love in your words, deeds and actions.
2. Let "love" overshadow fear.
3. Speak words of courage and faith
4. Read God's Word and pray together

Don't:

1. Don't buy love.
2. Don't put fear in your child by letting it be known that you are afraid.
3. Don't speak defeat by saying negative words.
4. Don't send your child to bed angry.

"You will show me the path that leads to life; for in your presence is fullness of joy..." Ps.16:11

Words/Phrases defined:

"art" – are.

"cast"- to toss it to; to roll it over on;
        release it

"'fear not" – don't fear; don't give in to
        fear; do not be afraid. You are not to
        have fear. You are not to be afraid.

"passeth" – surpasses; goes beyond.

"nought"- shall not be; as if it didn't
        exist/ never existed.

"saith" –   said; says.

"shalt" –   shall; will.

"thou" –   you.

My Observations:

____

____

____

____

____

____

____

____

____

____

More Observations:

We are applying these tools daily:

(say them out loud)

Applying More Tools:

Our results: ☺

Today,

____

____

____

____

____

____

____

____

____

____

Encourage children & youth to:

Avoid Strife. Don't fight!

Love! Don't hate.

Have faith! Not fear.

And always exchange good for evil!

And **forgive!**

Sharing is Love in Action:

Maybe you know a family whose child comes face-to-face with a bully every day or maybe you see a child who is afraid. So many lives have been lost, because parents and children did not have good information about bully prevention.

"Tips & Tools" could make a difference. You can be proactive about bully prevention by sharing information about this resource with other families. Let's work together to stop the bullying, to preserve future generations.

Consider purchasing a copy for another family who may not be able to afford it, and be a blessing.

More books by Patrice Lee:

"Mommie, R U Listening???" *
"Daddy! . . .Can YOU Hear Me???" *
"How to Overcome Every Obstacle...and Land on Top" *

"Bully Me? ...NO MORE!!!" (3rd – 7th grade)

"Bully Me?. . .NO MAS!!!" (en espanol)

"Bully Me? . . . Oh NO!!!" a TEEN Resource

"Happy to be Me!" (PreK – 2nd grade)
"The Bully Met My Dad!" (PreK- 3rd grade)
"Let's Love One Another" (PreK- 3rd grade)
It's Just a "CIRCUMSTANCE" (1st-5th grade)

For information on these and other books by Patrice Lee you may go to:
www.ucantbullyme.com
or email her at:
ucantbullyme@gmail.com

All books are available on Amazon.com

* Great books for adults

About the Author:

Patrice Lee experienced bullying in the workplace. However, she entered the workplace daily with a smile, a positive attitude and a willingness to do and be her best.

In Leep4Joy Books and Resources, she shares key ingredients needed to avoid the negative effects of bullying at school and work. She desires to see families "happy, healthy, and bully-free."

Each resource has encouraging words of faith, hope and love to help parents keep the home environment a bully-free-zone.

www.ingramcontent.com/pod-product-compliance
Lightning Source LLC
Chambersburg PA
CBHW051004050726
47592CB00007B/2692